ISBN-13: 978-1722893408
ISBN-10: 1722893400

This First Edition Published 2018.

Hare Publishing.

DEDICATION

For Peter, Jane, Rosie, Agata and Julia...

Thank you for your support.

Inspiration Quotes.

To those searching for Identity.
The Ocean is Calling you!

Long term happiness should be approached

sideways like a Crab.

"Just being Crab".

Written and Illustrated

By Nettie Forsyth

Book 1. Self reflection Story Series.

Crabs have external hard shells.

Crabs have vulnerable undersides.

You may not see it very often;

but it is there all the time.

MALE SAND CRAB
nettie

Crabs often have external threats.

Crabs can put up their defences very quickly.

It's a defence mechanism for self protection.

Crabs are also open and honest which can leave them vulnerable at times.

Crabs are very loyal to others.

Others find Crabs very trustworthy.

Crabs are protective, safe and caring of others.

·FIDDLER CRAB·
Nettie

Crabs quickly have fluidity in moulting its old shell and

making a new one.

A Crab grows itself all the time.

Nettie
MOULTING CRAB

Crabs are great survivors.

They adapt to their surrounds without the need for social copying or approval.

Crabs are very aware of themselves.

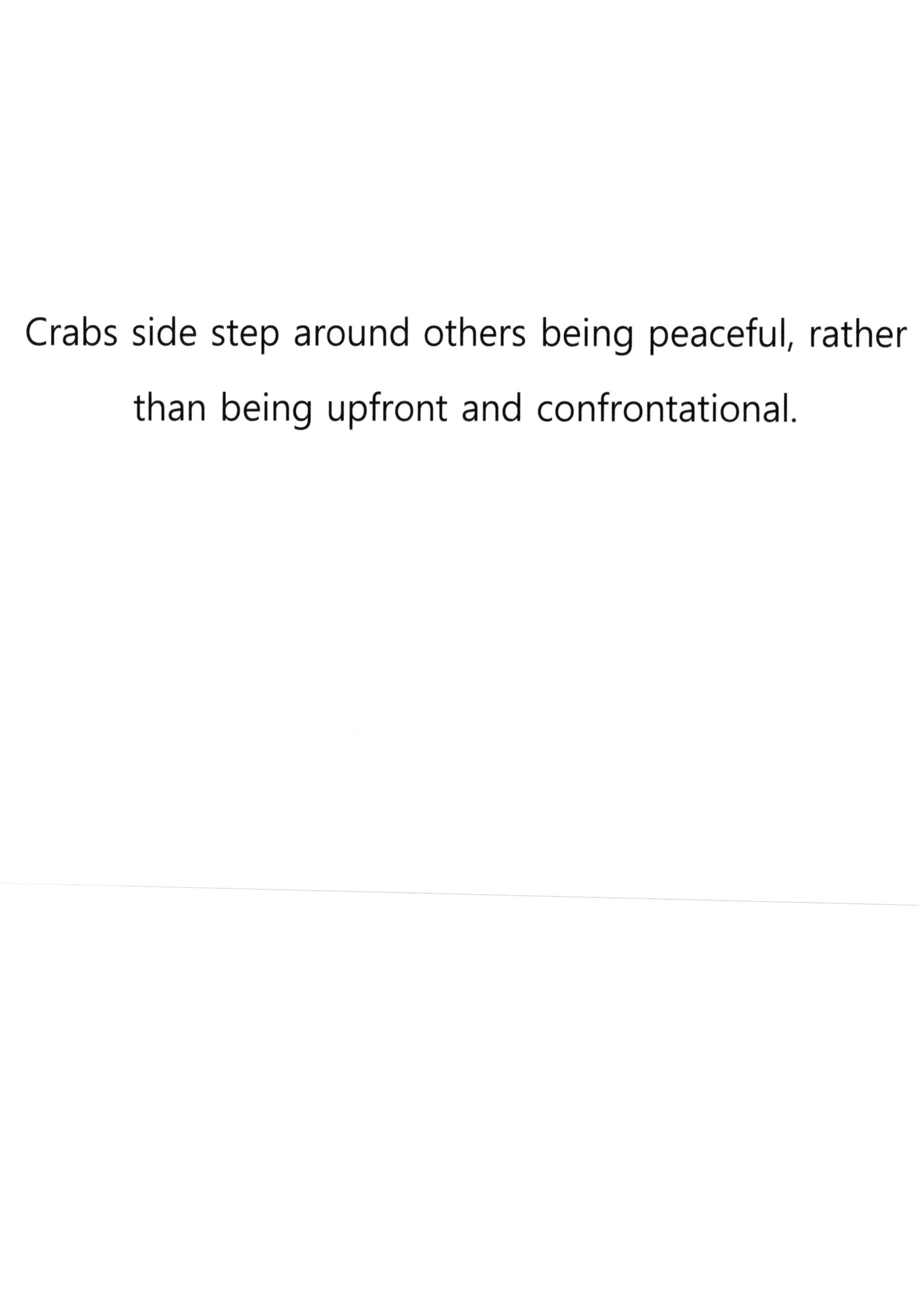

Crabs side step around others being peaceful, rather than being upfront and confrontational.

NETTIE

Crabs are very transparent, they are very authentic genuine creatures.

You get what you see.

There are no hidden agendas or character surprises.

Crabs know when to be noticed and when not to be noticed. They know when to blend in

Crabs are very observant and are happy to watch.

Crabs also know when to be bold and stand up for their beliefs.

They don't mind standing alone.

They don't always follow the crowd.

VELVET SWIMMING CRAB
NETTE

Crabs can be frequently contaminated by

environmental toxins.

They take on board those toxins, digest it, filter it;

giving it back with cleanliness.

Crabs are meticulous.

Crabs are organised.

They spend a lot of time cleaning and maintaining

themselves, their homes and their environments.

NETTIE
CLEANER CRAB

Crabs love being in and around water; it has a calming influence.

Water keeps the crab afloat in the stormiest of seas.

Crabs are survivors; Adapting to their surroundings and they like alone time and spending time on their own.

When Crabs feel relaxed and happy they like to play.

Crabs like to be arty.

Crabs are mainly balanced.

They manage the changing sands and the in and out tides.

BUBBLER CRAB
NETTIE
ND BALLS

Though it rarely happens, the worst thing about Crabs

is when they are pushed too far or feel threatened;

they can give you a little nip.

A warning to say stop, you've gone too far, its time to

back off and leave Crab alone .

Crabs can often be misunderstood; others can assume

a lot, and make the wrong assumptions!

Crabs have an ability to mask themselves easily; so

you would not know if the Crab is unhappy.

When life becomes overwhelming Crabs go quiet.

They hide in their shells until they feel more confident

to face the day.

HERMIT CRAB

Crabs just like being a Crab.

Hope you enjoyed learning some fun facts about

about Crabs!

ABOUT THE AUTHOR

Nettie Forsyth is a passionate advocate of Families, Children and Child development.

Known for her simplistic but vast knowledge base of Children, Child Development, Behaviour and Emotion work.

Nettie is appreciated by many she has worked with in her therapeutic Behaviour strategy and Counselling work.

Those who have had the privilege come away as very different people enabled and empowered.

The families functions and changes have been amazing within her work, whether it be child, siblings or parents.

Her Behaviour blog and common sense to parenting has empowered many parents.

As a parent herself got thrown into Adoption issues, SEN and Aspergers which bought its own learning. This was used as a learning tool and gave Nettie more insight in to the world of Challenging Behaviour.
Her own Daughter becoming a successful young adult.

This all inspires the books she writes.

Contacts:

Challenging-Behaviour@hotmail.co.uk

www.help-with-challenging-behaviour.co.uk

Other books by this Author and Illustrator.
Loveall & Spike
It's not okay!
Just being crab
Ellie's singing Tales